Until Debt Do Us Part
"The Workbook"

"The Day that Debt Died"

I0141102

"Now there cried a certain woman of the wives of the sons of the prophets unto Elisha, saying, Thy servant my husband is dead; and thou knowest that thy servant did fear the LORD: and the creditor is come to take unto him my two sons to be bondmen." 2 Kings 4:1

Apostle Lester Coward

UWriteit Publishing Company
Goldsboro, NC USA
www.uwriteitpublishingcompany.com
"Let us publish your book for you."

ISBN: **ISBN-13: 978-0615675497 (UWriteIt Publishing Company)**
ISBN-10: 0615675492

First Printing August – 2012

Unless otherwise indicated, Scripture quotations in this book are
from the King James Version of the Bible.

Dedication

I dedicate this book to my secretary Mrs. Annette Harper, a dedicated servant of the Lord.

Table of Contents

Introduction

1. Poor No More — **The Poor No More Check-up**
2. Until Debt Do Us Part — **The 30 Day Commitment**
3. Money Don't Live Here Anymore — **Assessing the Reasons Why**
4. A Financial Anointing — **The Foundations for Financial Freedom**
5. Giving and the Seed — **Getting to the Bottom of Things — Question and Answer Techniques**
6. Supernatural Money — **Some Common Core Beliefs**
7. Money Begets Money — **Things to Remember and Apply**

Introduction

If you have read the companion book of Until Debt Do Us Part then get ready to learn how to apply what you read through this workbook in order to manifest it in your life. The word of God says, *"Wisdom is the principal thing; therefore get wisdom: and with all thy getting get understanding."* Proverbs 4:7

Understanding is essential because it helps you to comprehend how to apply what you know to your everyday life and situations. With the proper understanding you will not simply have a head full of knowledge but you will have the knowhow to make that knowledge work for you.

Through this workbook you will learn many essential things that will make the difference between the person that just has the book and the person that has both the companion workbook and the book so that they can go to the next level in debt free living. In this workbook you will learn such things as:

- **The Poor No More Check-up**
- **The 30-Day Commitment**
- **Assessing Your Reasons Why Money Doesn't Live At Your House Anymore**
- **The Foundations for Financial Freedom**
- **Getting to the Bottom of Things—Question and Answer Techniques**

- **Some Common Core Beliefs**
- **Things to Remember and Apply**

Through this workbook the journey continues and Apostle Coward will show you how to get from where you are to where you desire to be. Here is the workbook that is scripturally sound and will blast you from poverty to prosperity and from debt to debt free living. You are a child of God and it's time to rise from the basement to the big league and from the poorhouse to the rich house. You are a child of the King and it's time to start living like it and this workbook is the starting point for your financial success. Throughout the workbook you will find space where answers can be written directly in the book, you will come across such work as questions and answers, yes or no answers, definitions, etc… all designed to help bring structure in your financial life. The answers to these questions, definitions, solutions, etc… are in the book **"Until Debt Do Us Part."** The best method is to do one chapter a day thereby concluding the book in one week. You will also learn about the 30-day commitment that will instruct you to commit to reading and applying these principles for one month. This workbook is a training tool and it contains instructions and exercises designed to equip you to come out of debt so that *"you can spend the rest of your days in prosperity and your years in pleasure."* Job 36:11

Beginning Prayer: Father, I thank you for the opportunity to learn the truth of your word about debt cancellation. I realize that I am a child of God and it's time for me to rise from the basement to the big league in my financial life. As I go forth to read and apply the knowledge that I am receiving I thank you for understanding; for you said with all my getting get understanding and I thank you now that the eyes of my understanding are being enlightening from this day forward and I thank you for your grace to be committed to the things in this workbook and the results that I shall receive because you are faithful that promised and I receive it now in Jesus name, amen.

1

Poor No More

"Save when there shall be no poor among you; for the LORD *shall greatly bless thee in the land which the* LORD *thy God giveth thee for an inheritance to possess it: Only if thou carefully hearken unto the voice of the* LORD *thy God, to observe to do all these commandments which I command thee this day." Deuteronomy 15:4-5*

As a Christian God doesn't want you down and out, God wants you to have an abundant life. You were born to be blessed with the best. If you are a child of God you don't have to be poor. The bible says, *"the poor you will have with you always and the poor will never cease." Mark 14:7, Deuteronomy 15:11* But you don't have to be one of the poor. Out of the ashes I rise, God wants to get you out of the ashes. Here are some things about the poor.

- *Wealth maketh many friends; but the poor is separated from his neighbor. Proverbs 19:4*
- *The poor is hated even of his own neighbor: but the rich hath many friends. Proverbs 14:20*

Some people are poor by choice and want to be poor. You got to pull yourself out of that poor mentality. Low and humble is the way, but you don't have to stay low. Sometimes you hear people say we were always poor and nobody in our family had anything, well it is time for you to reverse the curse.

You were born to taste the grapes and wine and have some oil. When you get born again you are a royal child, born into royalty, broke no more and poor no more. The struggle is over; your attitude must be **"I am not struggling anymore."**

God wants you to have money to do things with. Two broke people and two poor people cannot help each other. You were born to have some money!

THE POOR NO MORE CHECK-UP

It's time to take a check up from the neck up and see where your thinking is and why you're not where you want to be financially. You must answer these questions honestly and seriously, you must first be honest with yourself and come to a realization of where you are and why you're there.

1. Are you living a life of lack in the financial area of your life? Yes_____ or No_____

2. Why are you in financial lack? _____

   _____

   _____

   _____

3. Do you believe that God want you down and out and living a life of lack and debt? Yes _____

or No _____. What kind of life do you believe God wants you to live? _____

_____

_____

4. Why are people poor? _____

_____

5. What do people have to do to come out of poverty? _____

_____

6. What kind of attitude must you have to break free of poverty? _____

_____

_____

7. Were you born to have some money or born to be poor? _____

_____

_____

8. Can God trust you with money? Yes____ or No _____? Read Acts 5: 1-11 What did you get out of this story? _____

_____

_____

_____

_____

9. What happens when God blows on your money? _____

_____

_____

_____

_____

10. Who does all the money in the world belong to and what do you have to do as a saint to get some of it in your hands? _____

_____

_____

_____

_____

_____

_____

_____

Conclusion: If your first two answers are in the negative then you're in the poorhouse and in debt because of your negative thinking. You have stinking thinking and if you want to come out of debt then you must begin to change your thinking from this day forward. **No more excuses, you must change now! Read chapter 1 in the book over again.**

Prayer for Today: Father, I thank you that I am poor no more. As a Christian you don't want me down and out, you want me to live an abundant life. Jesus came that I might have life and that I will have it more abundantly. I am a royal child born into royalty and I am not struggling anymore. I rebuke the demon of hard times and I claim my rightful inheritance as a child of God. Father, all the money belongs to you for your word says, *"The earth is the LORD'S, and the fullness thereof; the world, and they that dwell therein." Psalms 24:1* I thank you for placing an anointing on me to profit and show the world how you have blessed me since I received you in Jesus name, amen.

2

Until Debt Do Us Part

"Now there cried a certain woman of the wives of the sons of the prophets unto Elisha, saying, Thy servant my husband is dead; and thou knowest that thy servant did fear the LORD: and the creditor is come to take unto him my two sons to be bondmen. Then she came and told the man of God. And he said, Go, sell the oil, and pay thy debt, and live thou and thy children of the rest." 2 Kings 4:1, 7

In the marriage vow it says until death do us part. It is saying we will stay together until one of us dies, until death do us part. There are so many people bound by debt and don't see no way out. There is a way that debt can depart, have faith in God to send a money anointing in your life. God want you out of debt and able to pay for what you get.

You don't want to live all your life with debt hanging over your head. People will stay together as long as things are going well. You need to layaway things when you don't have the money to pay.

Don't settle for having debts all of your life. Look for your money condition to get better.

Debts Up To My Neck

"And it shall come to pass in that day, that his burden shall be taken away from off thy shoulder, and his yoke from off thy neck, and the yoke shall be destroyed because of the anointing." Isaiah 10:27

"Though he heap up silver as the dust, and prepare raiment as the clay; He may prepare it, but the just shall put it on, and the innocent shall divide the silver." Job 27:16-17

It's time to break and destroy the debts from around your neck. It will take a supernatural anointing to do it. When you are up to your neck in debts it is hard to breathe so to speak. Debt is a spirit and we get carried away with it, it feels good at the time but when the bills begin to roll in that's when the trouble begins.

God has released his financial anointing (take it). People that are saved see no way out; it will take the anointing to get you out. It is bad to be yoked up with debts so that you can't even sleep. We need to destroy that yoke with the anointing. Your spirit is crying inside of you saying get me out of all this debt.

God is sending an end-time anointing to be released in the saints debts. You must receive this anointing in your spirit to come out of debt. You can't borrow your way out of debt; God will do it supernaturally with a divine intervention. One thing you must understand is that God will use me in prophecy and the prophetic to get you out of your money trouble, believe the prophet, *"believe his prophets, so shall ye prosper." 2 Chronicles 20:20*

Faith in God will pull you through and pull you out

of debt. Say, **"For me the anointing is on me and I wear it well."** Command the demon of debt to be rebuked off of your life right now. We must declare war on this debt demon and pay cash for what we buy. If you can't pay for it wait until you get the money.

Join the Debt Free Army. We are choking up to our neck in debt; listen to what the Holy Ghost is saying through the anointing to you. Break that yoke from around your neck. When you are up to your neck in debt it means that there is no way out. But our God is able to destroy that yoke with the anointing. The anointing will break and destroy that yoke when the prophet is packing an anointing to get you out of debt. God will send a debt cancelling anointing. It will take money or cash to buy corn beef hash.

THE 30-DAY COMMITMENT

People that are in debt has made a commitment to debt, if you want to come out you must make a new commitment to debt free living. That commitment will consist of a 30-day commitment to debt no more. Let's begin the journey to commit to a change in your thinking, in your speaking and in your actions by applying this workbook for the next 30 days.

1. When two people get married what is the vow that they take and what does it mean?

_____

_____

_____

_____

_____

2. Did you take a vow to be with debt for the rest of your life? Yes _____ or No _____ Are you seriously ready to break free from your attachment with debt? Yes _____ or No _____ Are you ready to make the 30-day commitment? Yes _____ or No _____

3. I _____ (**sign your name here**), am making a commitment for the next 30-days to commit to changing my way of thinking, my way of talking and all actions that are contrary to debt free living. **Date:** _____

4. What will it take to break and destroy the debt from around your neck? _____

_____

_____

5. What will faith in God do for you? _____

_____

_____

What must you begin to say and command to happen in your life in order to come out of debt? _____

_____

_____

_____

_____

_____

6. When you become a part of the debt free army what does the anointing do and what kind of anointing will God send in your life?

_____

_____

_____

_____

_____

7. There are people in the bible that had debt but God gave them a debt cancellation and paid their bills off. There are three things you must know to be debt free what are they?

_____

_____

_____

8. Read Nehemiah 5:1-12 in the book on page 20-21. What did you get out of "**A Nation That Became Debt Free?**" _____

_____

_____

_____

_____

_____

9. Read Matthew 17:24-27 in the book on page 21. What did you get out of **"Jesus Had a Debt Cancellation?"** _____

_____

_____

_____

_____

_____

10. God is a debt cancelling God therefore what are 3 things you must stop doing immediately?

_____

_____

_____

_____

_____

For the next 30-days change your way of talking, stop all negative talking and negative thinking. Begin to apply what you are learning in this workbook for the next 30-days and watch what God will do in your life because of your commitment. You will find different words of expression in the book, begin to say those things on a daily basis for the next 30-day.

Conclusion: God wants to impregnate you with a spirit of debt cancellation and turn your gloom into glory. Keep sowing for your deliverance, give what you've never given before-$200, $300, $400, $500, $600, $700, you need to learn how to stretch your faith.

Saints want something for nothing, to get something you've never had before; you must do something you've never done. **Read chapter 2 in the book over again.**

Prayer for Today: Father, any vow that I have made with debt in the past I break it now in the name of Jesus. I refuse to live my life with debt hanging over my head. I thank you now for that supernatural anointing that breaks and destroys debt from around my neck. I receive that financial anointing now that is released in this end-time. I believe in the LORD my God, therefore I shall be established; I believe his prophets, so shall I prosper. Father, I thank you for putting me on the path to pay off all my debts and I am going debt free this year. I am now part of the debt free army and I am out of debt. I am now impregnated with a spirit of debt cancellation and you have turned my gloom into glory in Jesus name, amen.

3

Money Don't Live Here Anymore

"Ye looked for much, and, lo it came to little; and when ye brought it home, I did blow upon it. Why? saith the LORD *of hosts. Because of mine house that is waste, and ye run every man unto his own house." Haggai 1:9*

"The blessing of the LORD, *it maketh rich, and he addeth no sorrow with it." Proverbs 10:22*

Money has taken a vacation from your house, money don't live here anymore. It left your house when you fail to believe God for money. God wants you blessed, some time you may go and try to find a person that live at an address that you were told and you found out that they have moved.

Well, money will leave your house when you don't know how to handle money. Money will walk out on you and leave you holding the bag. Unpaid bills will cause money to walk out on you and make you lose what you had. **Money doesn't live here anymore.**

Money abandoned you and walked out on you, money went across town to somebody else house that could handle it. **Money doesn't live here anymore.**

Money is like a married man that will walk out on his wife. The reason money left your house is because you don't know how to handle your money. **Lord**

teach me how to be a money handler. Sometimes a woman will tell other women that Henry walked out on me, well when you fail to pay your tithes, money will walk out on you and leave your house and all you will be able to say is, **money doesn't live here anymore.**

Insufficient Funds

"Not that we are sufficient of ourselves to think any thing as of ourselves; but our sufficiency is of God." 2 Corinthians 3:5

"The LORD is my shepherd; I shall not want." Psalms 23:1

Sometimes you will get a return check back saying insufficient funds, meaning that you don't have enough money in the bank to cover the check. God is more than enough and he wants you to have an overflow of money in your bank account. God want you to have seed to sow, therefore you need faith for an overflow of money. God has placed an anointing on you that money will be attracted to you. In Psalms 23 it says, *"The LORD is my shepherd; I shall not want. He maketh me to lie down in green pastures: he leadeth me beside the still waters. He restoreth my soul: he leadeth me in the paths of righteousness for his name's sake. Yea, though I walk through the valley of the shadow of death, I will fear no evil: for thou art with me; thy rod and thy staff they comfort me. Thou preparest a table before me in the presence of mine enemies: thou anointest my head with oil; my cup runneth over. Surely goodness and mercy shall follow me all the days of my life: and I will dwell in the house of the LORD for ever."*

You may not write a check to someone and it bounce but you can be low in your money matters. The word of God teaches us that if we bless somebody we will reap a harvest. The bank of heaven is not broke or going broke. You can draw blessings from God that will supply your every need. There is no lack or slack in God, the Lord is your shepherd and there is no want in him.

Increase is running you down looking to give to you. God wants to pour out more than enough into your life; in this supernatural hour that we're in God will intervene on your behalf to give you more than enough. The Lord knows what you have need of before you ask and it is the will of God that you have money to pay every bill and then some left over.

ASSESSING THE REASONS WHY MONEY DON'T LIVE AT YOUR HOUSE

1. Are you a consistent tither? Yes _____ or No _____.

2. Do you truly believe God for money or do you doubt most of the time?

_____

_____

_____

3. Are you a good money handler? Yes _____ or No _____.

4. Are you constantly experiencing a lot of unpaid bills? Yes _____ or No _____.

5. Do you believe that debt is a thief and a demon? Yes _____ or No_____.

6. Are you constantly buying things on credit? Yes _____ or No _____.

7. Are you willing to make God a vow that you will pay for what you buy from now on and stop borrowing to buy things? Yes _____ or No _____.

8. Do you find yourself constantly robbing Peter to pay Paul? Yes _____ or No _____.

9. Do you believe that money has taken a vacation from your house and doesn't

live there anymore? Yes _____ or No
_____.

10. Do you truly believe that God wants you
blessed without a doubt? Yes _____ or No
_____.

Conclusion: People are working hard to pay off bills
and come out of debt, but you must trust God to get
you out. When he gets you out then you're out and
you don't owe man anything. **Read chapter 3 in the
book over again.**

Prayer for Today: Father, I ask you to make me a
money handler so that I can handle money skillfully.
I confess today that you are my Shepherd and I shall
not want. The bank of heaven is not broke or going
broke and there is no lack or slack in God. Increase is
running me down now and looking to give to me.
Father, I thank you that every bill is paid with some
left over. I rebuke the demon of debt and it will never
control me ever again, I am debt free in Jesus name
and money now lives in my house, amen.

4

A Financial Anointing

"Be not deceived; God is not mocked: for whatsoever a man soweth, that shall he also reap. For he that soweth to his flesh shall of the flesh reap corruption; but he that soweth to the Spirit shall of the Spirit reap life everlasting. And let us not be weary in well doing: for in due season we shall reap, if we faint not." Galatians 6:7-9

It is important that you sit under a leader that teaches with an anointing about money or finances. If we are to reap a money harvest we must sow seeds. Saints are looking for increase in their money but they never sow money. Give your money an assignment by naming what you want God to do for you in return for your seed.

Plant a specific seed for a specific need. You should live with expectation.

- Expectation is the powerful current that makes the seed work for you. *"But without faith it is impossible to please him: for he that cometh to God must believe that he is, and that he is a rewarder of them that diligently seek him." Hebrews 11:6*

- Expect protection as he promised. *"And I will rebuke the devourer for your sakes, and he shall not destroy the fruits of your ground; neither shall your vine cast her fruit before the time in the field, saith* the LORD of hosts." Malachi 3:11

- Expect favor from a Boaz close to you. *"Give, and it shall be given unto you; good measure, pressed down, and shaken together, and running over, shall men give into your bosom. For with the same measure that ye mete withal it shall be measured to you again."* Luke 6:38

- Expect financial ideas and wisdom from God as a harvest. *"But thou shalt remember the LORD thy God: for it is he that giveth thee power to get wealth, that he may establish his covenant which he sware unto thy fathers, as it is this day."* Deuteronomy 8:18

- Expect your enemies to fragment and be confused and flee before you. *"The LORD shall cause thine enemies that rise up against thee to be smitten before thy face: they shall come out against thee one way, and flee before thee seven ways."* Deuteronomy 28:7

- Expect God to bless you for every act of obedience. *"And it shall come to pass, if thou shalt hearken diligently unto the voice of the Lord thy*

God, to observe and to do all his commandments which I command thee this day, that the LORD thy God will set thee on high above all nations of the earth: And all these blessings shall come on thee, and overtake thee, if thou shalt hearken unto the voice of the LORD thy God." Deuteronomy 28:1-2

Reach up and grab what you're expecting and pull it down. People are not experiencing increase because no one has told them about the principle of seed faith. The unlearned are simply the untaught, teachers are necessary therefore you must sit at the feet of a teacher to learn. Everyone understand sowing and how to sow for a harvest.

- Seed faith is sowing a specific seed in faith that it will grow.
- Seed faith is letting go of something you have been given to create something else you have been promised.

Your seed is what blesses someone else, give your seed an assignment and it will bless the place where it is sown and will come back multiplied and bless you also.

The Foundations for Financial Freedom

In order to break free from debt and come into financial freedom you must build upon a solid and stable foundation that is absolute and that will work every time. In this chapter there are three things you must apply in order to experience debt free living and come into the supernatural that God has designed for your life. These three things are financial foundation stones and if you will apply them you will begin to see the financial anointing manifesting in your life. The three things for debt free living are:

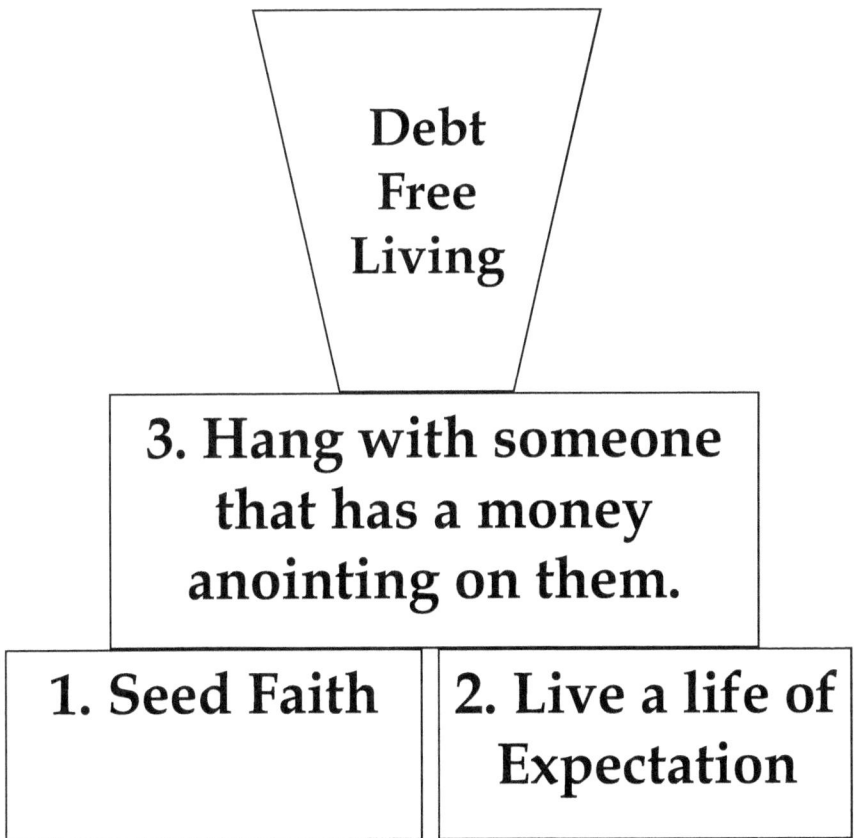

**Debt
Free
Living**

**3. Hang with someone
that has a money
anointing on them.**

1. Seed Faith

**2. Live a life of
Expectation**

1. What is the most important thing you must do in order to get a financial anointing? _____

    _____

    _____

    _____

    _____

2. In order to reap a money harvest what must you begin to do and what are saints looking for yet they never do? _____

    _____

    _____

3. What is a money assignment and why do you plant a specific seed? _____

    _____

    _____

    _____

    _____

    _____

    _____

4. What is seed faith? _____

    _____

    _____

    _____

    _____

5. Read Deuteronomy 28: 1-2. What stood out to you in these scriptures? _____

_____

_____

_____

_____

6. Read Genesis 13: 1-10. What stood out to you in these scriptures? _____

_____

_____

_____

_____

7. Why is it important to hang with someone that has a financial anointing on them? _____

_____

_____

_____

_____

_____

_____

8. Why is the seed so important? _____

_____

_____

_____

_____

9. Write out Luke 6:38. _____

_____

_____

_____

_____

10. Why should you live with expectation? _____

_____

_____

_____

_____

_____

_____

_____

_____

Conclusion: As a believer you need to hang with people that have some money, people that has a money anointing on them. Hang with somebody that can take you to the next level. Hang with the prophet that's packing a money anointing on them. If you are going to hang with somebody hang around blessed people that got something to offer. **Read chapter 4 in**

the book over again.

Prayer for Today: Father, thank you for a financial anointing over my life now. I reach up and grab what I need now in Jesus name. As I plant a specific seed I give my seed an assignment to go forth and create a supernatural harvest. I expect my seed to produce, I expect protection, I expect favor from a Boaz close to me, I expect financial ideas and wisdom from you, I expect my enemies to be fragment and be confused before me and I expect you to bless me for obedience to your word. You said *"But thou shalt remember the LORD thy God: for it is he that giveth thee power to get wealth, that he may establish his covenant which he sware unto thy fathers, as it is this day."* Deuteronomy 8:18 Thank you for my seed producing a harvest as I live a life of expectation and thank you for blessing me to hang with people that has a money anointing on them in Jesus name, amen.

5

Giving and the Seed

"Give, and it shall be given unto you; good measure, pressed down, and shaken together, and running over, shall men give into your bosom. For with the same measure that ye mete withal it shall be measured to you again." Luke 6:38

If you give you will get, your gift will return to you in full and overflowing measure, pressed down, shaken together to make room for more and running over. Whatever measure you use to give, large or small will be used to measure what is given back to you.

Check your giving and see if what you're giving is what you want to receive. The scripture says, *"Give, and it shall be given unto you; good measure, pressed down, and shaken together, and running over, shall men give into your bosom. For with the same measure that ye mete withal it shall be measured to you again." Luke 6:38*

When you give little don't look for much. You must learn to take on the mindset of the farmer and observe their way of sowing much seed to get back an abundance of crop. When you sow little you will reap little, your measure of giving will determine the measure that you will reap. Whatever you put out will come back in the manner that you put it forth.

Individuals want to reap abundance but they're not willing to give abundantly. But in order to reap abundantly you must give in abundance. God want to send you the abundant blessing, pressed down, shaken together and running over that man will bless you real good. Become a giver and make giving a habit and your giving will open unexpected doors for you. When you give favor will rest upon you. This is your season and its harvest time for you.

When you have a running over blessing then you can bless somebody else. In this hour when people are talking about recession, as a child of God you can talk about how bless you are. Don't stop your giving, intensify your giving and watch God supercharge your finances.

Your Seed Is Anointed to Grow

"That in blessing I will bless thee, and in multiplying I will multiply thy seed as the stars of the heaven, and as the sand which is upon the sea shore; and thy seed shall possess the gate of his enemies." Genesis 22:17

I want you to know that your seed is like money in the bank, when your money is in the bank it draws interest. Your seed when given to God will grow and multiply. You may ask how my seed is anointed to grow. After you have given your seed and it has left your hands doors are open and healing takes place. Increase begins to come your way and miracle money shows up for you. When your seed is anointed to grow you begin to see the suddenly of God.

Getting to the Bottom of Things — Question and Answer Techniques

1. Have you sowed a financial seed lately? Yes _____ or No _____.

2. What is the biggest financial seed that you have ever sown? _____

   _____

   _____

3. Check your giving and see if what you're giving is what you want to receive. Is it? Yes _____ or No _____.

4. Can you receive much if you are sowing little? Yes _____ or No _____.

5. What must you do if you want to receive much? _____

   _____

   _____

6. Does fear come upon you when you think about sowing a large seed? Yes _____ or No _____.

7. Has God given you a spirit of fear? Yes _____ or No _____.

8. Do you know what to do to break that spirit of fear that is holding you back from sowing a large seed? Yes _____ or No _____. In order to break that spirit of fear you must sow that large seed and believe God's word that you shall reap.

9. Do you know what happens after you give your seed? _____

   _____

   _____

   _____

   _____

10. Have you ever read the story about the widow woman that gave to Elijah the prophet? What is your true feeling about that? 1 Kings 17:8-16__

   _____

   _____

   _____

   _____

   _____

   _____

   _____

Conclusion: When God talks to you about a seed he has a harvest on his mind for you. Your money is anointed to grow and when your money is anointed it will go a long way. God will stretch your money and keep you from getting down to your last dime because your money is anointed to grow. **Read chapter 5 in the book over again.**

Prayer for Today: Father, thank you for your faithfulness and I know that your word will not go out and return void. You said, *"Give, and it shall be given unto you; good measure, pressed down, and shaken together, and running over, shall men give into your bosom. For with the same measure that ye mete withal it shall be measured to you again."* Luke 6:38 Father, I thank you for a running over blessing so much that I will be able to be a blessing to others. I thank you that my seed is anointed to grow and I am now experiencing the suddenly of God. My seed is anointed to grow with an increase on it. I thank you now for the harvest that you have on your mind and I shall never be broke another day in my life in Jesus name, amen.

6

Supernatural Money

"Notwithstanding, lest we should offend them, go thou to the sea, and cast an hook, and take up the fish that first cometh up; and when thou hast opened his mouth, thou shalt find a piece of money: that take, and give unto them for me and thee." Matthew 17:27

When you give you set yourself up for a miracle. When you obey God in your giving he is trying to get something to you. The more you give the more you will have. God has some miracle money coming your way, money that you have not worked for, miracle money.

In a pack of M&M's there are different colors, that is saying all kinds of money, 10, 20, 30, 40, 50, 60, 70, 80, 1000.00, 2000.00. Speak out into the atmosphere and say **"more money"**, it's not a sin to have money but the lack of money is a sin.

Don't let anybody talk you out of your blessing. Money will cause God to work great miracles in your life. Give and the more you give men will give unto you. We need miracle money, money that God will send your way from sources, peoples and places that you weren't looking for it from. God wants you to have millionaire faith and he wants to put you in a wealthy place.

A Lump Sum Miracle

"Though he heap up silver as the dust, and prepare raiment as the clay. He may prepare it, but the just shall put it on, and the innocent shall divide the silver." Job 27:16-17

"Thou preparest a table before me in the presence of mine enemies: thou anointest my head with oil; my cup runneth over." Psalms 23:5

A Lump Sum is an amount of money given in a single payment or things that equate to money. I want you to know that God got a lump sum of miracle money for you. This is the time for a money release that is on the way for you, have faith for a lump sum. With God the unexpected can happen anytime, there are people in the Bible that got a lump sum from God.

Job in the Bible lost everything that he had but when God blessed him again he received a lump sum return. If you want to get a lump sum from God you must sow a seed toward your lump sum. God is ready to give you the hundred fold blessing. Mark 10:28-31

Abraham had a lump sum anointing on his life, the lump sum anointing that was on Abraham fell on Lot to the point that he had so much that he had to go to another city.

Some Common Core Beliefs

Many times people have some common core beliefs that are ingrained into their mind and spirit. These beliefs have become a part of their innermost person and often times chart the course of their destiny. These core beliefs have to be debunked before any major changes can be made. In this chapter we want to help you eradicate every core belief that is contrary to sound biblical scripture and prosperity living and we will do this through the word of God. The scripture says, *"For the word of God is quick, and powerful, and sharper than any twoedged sword, piercing even to the **dividing asunder** of soul and spirit, and of the joints and marrow, and is a discerner of the thoughts and intents of the heart." Hebrews 4:12*

Some Common Core Belief Statements

- *Some people are not supposed to prosper in life.*
- *My family has always been poor so that means I will probably be poor also.*
- *You have to know someone important to prosper.*
- *Something is wrong with me I wasn't born to be rich.*
- *I'm not good enough or smart enough I am destined for a life of barely making ends meet.*
- *Only certain people are supposed to prosper in life.*
- *You can't be honest and get ahead in this world.*

The main cause of these core beliefs are a negative attitude and wrong beliefs about your life. Many individuals see their life through what they believe and if the core of their belief is negative then their belief about their financial life will be pessimistic and doubtful. In order to change your attitude you must first change your core belief.

1. What is your core belief about prosperity?

   _____

   _____

   _____

   _____

   _____

2. Do you have any of the most common core beliefs listed above? Yes _____ or No _____ Which of the beliefs do you have and why do you think you have them?

   _____

   _____

   _____

   _____

   _____

   _____

3. When you give, what does it set you up for and what is God trying to do through your giving? _____

_____

_____

4. Do you believe in miracles? Yes _____ or No _____. How do you get miracle money? _____

_____

_____

_____

_____

5. What kind of faith does God want you to have? _____

_____

_____

6. What is a Lump Sum and name two people that received a Lump Sum?

_____

_____

_____

_____

_____

_____

_____

7. Write out these two scriptures, 2 Chronicles 20:20 and Isaiah 7:9.

_____

_____

_____

_____

_____

_____

8. Miracles happen to people that are expecting them, name 7 ways that miracles happen. _____

_____

_____

_____

_____

_____

_____

9. Do you believe that God can catch your bills up supernaturally? Yes _____ or No _____. Speak out of your mouth this confession on a daily basis: **My bills are paid off now in Jesus Name!**

10. Recognize that God is your supernatural provider. This thought must become a core belief in your mind and spirit. Name 7 ways that God is your supernatural provider. _____

_____

_____

_____

_____

_____

_____

Lift up your hands and say, *"All my needs are met and all my bills are paid now."*

Conclusion: Trust the Lord today and see doesn't he make a way because he is a way maker. We must learn to get off the **world system** and get on the **word system**. If you are a child of God you will be provided for by your heavenly Father. All of your needs are met and God will not let you go under before he will let you go over. God is your helper and he will make a way out of no way for you. **Go back and read chapter 6 in the book over again.**

Know that your help is on the way.

Prayer for Today: Father, I thank you for supernatural money because I believe that you are a miracle working God. You are the same yesterday, today and forever and you change not. You are the same God that did amazing occurrences and supernatural provisions throughout the scriptures. I believe that you want me to have millionaire faith and that you want to put me in a wealthy place. I confess that I need miracle money now, money that you will send my way from sources, people and places that I wasn't looking for it from. I believe in a Lump Sum miracle and that the unexpected can and will happen for me now. I feel a lump sum anointing working its way toward me now in Jesus name. Father, I thank you that my bills are paid off and help is on the way now. Thank you for being a very present help in the time of need, *"So that we may boldly say, The Lord is my helper, and I will not fear what man shall do unto me." Hebrews 13:6* In Jesus name, amen.

7

Money Begets Money

"Wealth maketh many friends; but the poor is separated from his neighbour." Proverbs 19:4

I hear money calling your name, money is looking for you. Money draws money and God want to make you a money magnet. The more you give it comes back to you in double abundance. The anointing will cause money to come your way, God will move on somebody supernaturally to give you some money. Let me hear you say, **"I Feel Money Coming."**

It's on me and I wear it well, what's on me, a money anointing. Money is on its way to your address, look for it in your mail box, miracle money is being released your way. God wants to work for you, *"It is time for thee, LORD, to work: for they have made void thy law." Psalms 119:126* If you want more money then you must watch your words, *"Thou art snared with the words of thy mouth, thou art taken with the words of thy mouth."Proverbs 6:2*

I want you to know that you will reap money when you give it, *"The desire of the righteous is only good: but the expectation of the wicked is wrath. There is that scattereth, and yet increaseth; and there is that withholdeth more than is meet, but it tendeth to poverty. The liberal soul shall be made fat: and he that watereth shall be watered also himself." Proverbs 11:23-25*

It is all right to love people but love doesn't pay any bills. You can't go to the electric company and tell them, *"I don't have the money to pay my bill this month but I love you"* or go to your phone company and tell them *"I know my bill is due this month but I don't have the money but I just want you to know that I love you all."* They will look at you like you are crazy; you must go to these companies with the m-o-n-e-y.

You must begin to stretch your faith and begin to give $50, $75, $100 and even a $1,000. It will take the anointing to get you out of your debts. God will use somebody that will show you favour. When God bless you with money there is a mission that he uses for his kingdom. The giving anointing is working in you and when you sow expect a great harvest. Money with a mission to send the gospel throughout the whole earth so that souls can be saved set free and delivered.

Things to Remember and Apply

1. Repeat this phrase daily as often as possible: **I FEEL MONEY COMING NOW!!!**

2. Speak the word that will bring about a change in your financial life — **Money Cometh to Me Now!**

3. If you are a child of God there is an anointing on you for money, lift your hands and say **"Money is coming to these hands now."**

4. I hear money calling your name, money is looking for you. Money draws money and God want to make you a money magnet. The more you give it comes back to you in double abundance. The anointing will cause money to come your way, God will move on somebody supernaturally to give you some money.

5. You must begin to stretch your faith and begin to give $50, $75, $100 and even a $1,000. It will take the anointing to get you out of your debts.

6. What does **"Stand on Your Money Confession"** mean? _____
   _____
   _____
   _____
   _____

7. Speak into the atmosphere right now and say, **"Money I hear you knocking, so come on in."**

8. Finish these 3 phrases by writing them out.
Money is _____.
Millions and _____.
God doesn't want you _____

_____

_____.

9. Write out the definition of these phrases.
Miracle Money: _____
Have Money to Burn: _____

_____

_____

In the Money: _____

_____

_____

Make Money: _____

_____

_____

Money Magnet: _____

_____

_____

Money Coming to Me: _____

_____

_____

On the Money: _____

_____

_____

10. **There is a money anointing on you receive it now!** Do you believe this wholeheartedly? Yes _____ or No _____.

Conclusion: Your breakthrough for more money is upon you right now. The devil has made many of the saints feeling like it is wrong to have money. God wants you to live a blessed life and have the things you desire. God is fed up with you advertising his kingdom broke, money draws money and God wants to raise you from the dunghill.

Money talk and broke folks walk. Money is getting ready to knock on your door. Money is ready to pay off all your bills!

We pray that this workbook has been a tremendous blessing to you in helping to renew your thinking and giving you a new mindset. Refer back to your workbook often and meditate upon the answers that you wrote out and the changes that you need to make to see the manifestations of financial increase, prosperity and wealth come into your life. You were born to represent the kingdom, not through lack and debt but in abundance and blessings. *"Fear not, little* *flock; for it is **your** Father's good pleasure to **give you the kingdom**."Luke 12:32* **Read chapter 7 in the book over again.**

Final Conclusive Prayer: Father, in the name of Jesus, I declare and decree that money is calling my name and looking for me now. The anointing will cause money to come my way and God I ask that you move upon somebody supernaturally to give me some money. I feel money coming, it's on me and I wear it well in Jesus name. My breakthrough for money is on me right now because you want me to live a blessed life and have the things I desire.

Father, I put my trust in you as Lord and provider, you are my supernatural source and I am expecting miraculous manifestations in my money now. I am expecting:

- Settlements
- Unexpected money
- Checks in the mail
- Refunds of all kinds
- Miracle money that I did not work for
- Hidden money
- Money for my eyes only

I thank you for debt cancellation and supernatural deliverance because you are a wonder worker. You are a way maker and I thank you for a Lump Sum blessing. Thank you Father for being my:

- Money provider
- My bill payer
- My house mortgage or rent provider
- My car note maker
- My light bill man
- My bread and meat provider and
- What you can't do just can't be done

There is a money anointing on me right now and I receive it. Money is knocking at my door, money I hear you knocking so come on in, in the mighty name of Jesus Christ the anointed one, I am blessed beyond measure and debt is no more in my life, in Jesus name amen.

www.ingramcontent.com/pod-product-compliance
Lightning Source LLC
LaVergne TN
LVHW021548080426
835509LV00019B/2901